Joseph Warren Alden

Vaticanism Unmasked : or, Romanism in the United States

Joseph Warren Alden

Vaticanism Unmasked : or, Romanism in the United States

ISBN/EAN: 9783744779326

Printed in Europe, USA, Canada, Australia, Japan

Cover: Foto ©Lupo / pixelio.de

More available books at **www.hansebooks.com**

VATICANISM UNMASKED,

OR,

ROMANISM

IN THE UNITED STATES.

BY

A PURITAN OF THE NINETEENTH CENTURY.

———•———

CAMBRIDGE, MASS.:

PUBLISHED BY THE PRINCIPIA CLUB.

POST-OFFICE ADDRESS, BOX 104.

1877.

PREFACE.

The papal church is a human institution which throws her sacerdotal robes over the whole civilized world. The Pope usurps the authority of Jesus Christ as the supreme head of the church militant on earth, and claims the right to rule the world in God's stead. This audacious claim is rigidly enforced in all parts of the world by military power, where the claim is disputed, and where there are bayonets enough to insure success, at the command of the vatican. In a Republic like this, diplomacy, strategy, intrigue and all manner of fraud and deception are used according to circumstances, until the civil power is under control, after which obedience to the supreme Pontiff is the law of the land. He usurps the prerogatives of both Christ and Cæsar. This arrangement is quite convenient, inasmuch as there is but one source of authority, and nobody is in danger, by transgressing Christ's command "render therefore unto Cæsar the things which are Cæsar's, and unto God the things that are God's." This is a logical sequence of papal supremacy and infallibility. Once established, one mind can rule the world from a single point to wit, the vatican at Rome. A syllabus ex-cathedra is better authority in the mind of a papist than a "thus saith the Lord" of the Bible. The Pope's bull of excommunication has more terrors in it than all the thunders of Sinai, and the penalties of God's broken laws.

These propositions may seem extravagant to those who have never examined the subject, but the reader will find them sustained in the following pages:

In the third decade of the present century, when fitting for college under a Jesuit priest, the writer was thoroughly instructed in the aims, plans and future prospects of the Roman Hierarchy, in this country, as well as in the doctrines of the papal church. During the last fifty years we have studied the nature and watched the progress of Romanism in this Republic, with intense interest, hoping to see some abler pen lay open its real character and designs to protestants of the nineteenth century.

In reading the histories of eighteen centuries it has become more and more apparent that the claims of the vatican to infallibility, to universal dominion, to an unbroken line of succession from the apostles, to the power of absolution from sin through time and eternity, are one and all stupendous humbugs, and the greatest frauds ever palmed off upon the human race.

To establish these blasphemous claims in these United States and territories, and upon this continent, is the work of the present century, by the Roman Hierarchy, through its cardinals, bishops and priests, as has been openly and boldly avowed by them from time to time.

It is the design of this pamphlet to lay open the true character of the institution which purposes to substitute despotism for republicanism in this country, and we have condensed the proofs from history so as to bring them within the reach of the protestant masses, before it shall be too late, to resist the encroachments of the papal power.

The histories to which we are chiefly indebted are "Millman's Latin Christianity," including the numerous authors quoted by him, both protestant and papal, to the "Period of the Reformation by Hausser," to the "Huguenots in France after the Revocation of the Edict of Nantes, by Samuel Smiles," to "D'Aubigne's History of the Reformation of the sixteenth century," and "A Synopsis of Popery as it was and as it is, by William Hogan, Esq., formerly Roman catholic priest."

After the first three centuries of the Christian era, satan was permitted to take possession of the church, as he was permitted to take Job in hand more than fifteen hundred years before. The pure gold of Christianity was soon buried in the rubbish of sacerdotal religion and christians were well nigh smothered into silence for more than a decade of centuries. But Jesus Christ had said of HIS church (not the Pope's) "the gates of hell shall not prevail against it," and after satan had had ample time to extinguish it, God arose in his power, dug out of that mountain of rubbish, the ore, separated the gold from the dross in his great refining-pot of free discussion, and set the current in another direction. John Wickliffe, John Huss, Jerome of Prague, Martin Luther, Melancthon, Zwingle and others were evidences that the great principles of christianity yet lived. Luther began the Reformation by attacking the papal system first in its corrupt practices and second in its doctrines. Pope Leo X. flattered, threatened, raged and bellowed in turn. His Bulls were issued and served as sandpaper to burnish the gold which had become dim by long disuse, until all Germany was lighted up with gospel fires. Luther, armed with the Bible, went out to battle with the supreme Pontiff and his legates as David with his sling and smooth stones gave battle to Goliath and the Philistines. The one was a moral, the other a physical power, with an Almighty arm to guide each.

Christendom has two systems of religion, Christianity and Hierarchism, from which to choose. God is the author of the first which is the only system that embraces human salvation. The priest is the author of the second, which is the system we shall lay open in this pamphlet, as delineated in history. In the hierarchial system, ecclesiastical *penance* was substituted for christian *repentance* in christianity. The translation of the new testament was altered to conform to this counterfeit of a great fundamental principle in christianity, which substituted the Roman Pontiff for Jesus Christ and placed the priest between the Creator and his creatures. In the protestant Bible *repentance* is an exercise of the *heart*, contrition for sin against God, and an act towards God. In the Douay testament *penance* is substituted for *repentance* contrary to the true rendering of the original Greek. This is the fundamental difference between protestantism and papacy.

We shall show that the Roman catholic church is the only institution in this world that claims infallibility, and that it is, of all others, the most corrupt, ungodly and despotic; and consequently it is no more entitled to the character of catholicity than satan it to that of saint.

We also propose to show from its own history that it has never reformed, that its character has been essentially the same for the last fourteen centuries, that when modified in its professions at all in any country, it has been only while getting possession of the civil power, as now in this Republic, and that the civil power when once in its hands has always been used to smother christianity and force christians into obedience to the demands of the vatican.

THE AUTHOR.

Cambridge, Mass., 1877.

CONTENTS.

CHAPTER I.

CHAPTER II.

CHAPTER III.

CHAPTER IV.

CHAPTER V.

CHAPTER VI.

VATICANISM UNMASKED.

CHAPTER I.

ROMANISM — CIVIL POWER — PROTESTANTISM.

The history of the Latin church from its apostacy from the true church in the fourth century, is a history of crimes committed under the garb of religion. The assumptions of its long lines of Popes to rule the world as vicegerents of God have succeeded in every country on the globe where the political power could be added to the ecclesiastical. In this country the papal power has not yet gained the victory, but it has already captured the outposts of protestantism, and while satan is singing to the protestant church the lullaby of *no danger*, the cunning papacy is making rapid strides to the very citadel of protestantism.

Their priests already claim that their church embraces within its folds a majority of the officers of the army and navy of the nation.

In another chapter we shall show, what the newspaper press has already published as items of news, that a very large majority of the police force of our principal cities are Roman Catholics, and we will add here for the consideration of our protestant friends, the patent fact that they are organizing military companies all over the land — building immense cathedrals in all the principal cities, and especially in the Southern States for the negroes.

But what are the scattered forces of the protestant church about all this time? They have had the civil power in their hands ever since the landing of the Pilgrims and the organization of this republic. Their sons seems to have forgotten what their fathers taught them, to wit, that "eternal vigilance is the price of liberty."

They are like a family of children quietly sleeping while the house over their heads is on fire, or while the lighted fuse is quietly burning its way to a powder magazine underneath it and them.

Thus the churches are sleeping on, while the papal forces under the supreme control of the vatican at Rome are intriguing for the possession of the civil power of this country, which means according to the most authentic histories of that church, the entire snuffing out and extinction of protestantism. That we do not overstate the case we appeal to history and beg our protestant friends to give the subject a thorough investigation. Two and a half centuries ago protestantism fled from the persecutions of the old world, and took possession of a howling wilderness on this continent, where they could worship God according to the dictates of their own consciences, with none but owls and Indians to molest or make them afraid. In process of time they constituted the Pulpit and the Press their watchmen and placed them on the watch towers of Zion to guard their liberties, and warn the people of their danger whenever it approached. Some twenty-three hundred years before that, under a theocracy, God revealed to his prophet Ezekiel the penalty a watchman incurred in not blowing the trumpet to warn the people of their danger when he saw the sword coming. These are his words: "But if the watchman see the sword come, and blow not the trumpet, and the people be not warned; if the sword come and take any person from among them, he is taken away in his iniquity; but his blood will I require at the watchman's hands." *Ezek.* 33: 6.

Watchman what of the night? Do you not see the papal sword glistening in the distance? If not, it is only because it is hid under the tinsel robes and gaudy trappings of the hierarchy, and wo to the watchman who does not blow his trumpet to warn the people of the approach of the enemy. We use the English language not to cover up crime, neither do we propose to tax our ingenuity to conceal great rascalities behind little "irregularities." The time has come to know who is for Christ and who for anti-Christ.

And now that the Protestant powers are uppermost in a large part of Europe and no longer under the control of the papal power she is pushing for this country, landing her forces by the thousand in New York, where naturalization papers await them and where they are at once transformed into voters, supplemented by Jesuits and sisters of charity by the ship-load, to instruct them in their duties to the dominant party of that democratic city. In this way she hopes to hold the balance of power between the two political parties, until by the power of majorities, at no distant day, she can capture this country and wield its immense resources and power in her own interest. A disturber everywhere she is making herself felt a disturber here. Her nature and history are one, and she will never rest until she has gained the ascendency in this country, and when that day comes the Republic, as our fathers framed it, and as her sons have administered it, is no more. These are grave charges and should not be lightly made. But we do make them under the following count, in proof of which we summon her own history.

1. Her claim of universal power, temporal and spiritual, in heaven and on earth, exalts her above all civil governments, in the eyes of her devotees.

2. Her attempt to seize and exercise this universal power, AS GOD ON EARTH!

3. This power disallows disagreement with her own dogmas, and enforces her authority with the death penalty, when and where she has military power enough to enforce it.

4. She has always sought alliance with the political powers to enforce her audacious claims.

5. She absolves her adherents from the duty of obeying the civil government in all cases when the government does not favor her schemes.

6. She instructs her adherents how to act, and how to *vote* on all matters touching her interests.

7. She is hostile to whatever is national and American in distinction to what is Roman catholic, to wit, free press, free speech, free schools, open bibles, a sacred Sabbath, &c.

8. She insists that her adherents shall in no way fraternize with protestant Americans, socially or religiously, nor imbibe the national spirit, and is bent on promoting among them clannishness, bigotry and intolerance, (catholic servants are not allowed to attend worship in protestant families or protestant meetings. The church demands separate schools, separate literary, benevolent and temperance societies.)

9. Her spirit has grown more intensely Romish and intolerant within the last twenty or thirty years than ever before in this country. Note the renewal of the Pope's

claim to Infallibility, its admission, his anathemas against those who reject it — Maryolotry — the Guibord burial case — church celebrations — their prior right to our streets on St. Patrick's day — church building, consecrations, &c.

10. She is always on the side of oppression as against republicanism and gives her influence and support to the party that will most aid her schemes and interests, as for instance the democratic party in New York — and the Southern rebels.

11. She makes no concealment of her purpose to take possession of this country, and rule it in the interests of Rome; e. g., "Father Hecker's" boast — his mission abroad to stir up catholic emigration to this country for the purpose of increasing the catholic vote — Her efforts in the south to capture the colored people after they were emancipated and made voters, and the poor whites whose stupid ignorance is the best qualification for papal rule — the boasts of the priests that they have now a majority of the army and navy officers.

12. Probable understanding between the southern leaders of the democratic party, and the leaders of the Catholic church, the politicians to help the church to *converts* and *spiritual* power, and the church to help the politicians to voters and political power. Note the speech of Jeff Davis at New Orleans, the Pope's special kindness during the war, and the reluctance to educate either race, except in church dogmas and military tactics.

THE AUTOCRACY AND DESPOTISM OF PAPACY — UNION OF CHURCH AND STATE — ECCLESIASTICAL AND CIVIL POWER COMBINED.

In the early part of the fourth century, under Constantine the Great, the papal power began to make more serious inroads upon the democracy of christianity. Two fearful strides were taken in that direction by the emperor, designedly or otherwise, to wit, 1st, the union of church and state under one supreme head, and 2d, the legal power given the papal church to hold real estate and other property in its own name. This opened the floodgates of corruption to such an extent that the supreme head of church and state on earth was hardly able to withstand it, and to which many of his successors implicitly yielded. This constituted the papal church, the great savings bank of the world, and confirmed its creed as the only legal christianity. Its financial condition was improved, at the expense of the revenues of the state. For several centuries its immense wealth was lavished in building cathedrals, monasteries and nunneries. The priest's office became lucrative, and corrupt men pressed into it. For hundreds of years bishoprics were bought and sold in the market with impunity, and simony was the rule and not the exception. The Pope was not only the supreme head of the church but commander-in-chief of the armies. His cardinals and archbishops were his field officers caparisoned with sword and spear, boot and spur, and his soldiers were his most effective instruments for the "conversion" of heretics at the point of the bayonet. Some of their exploits in this direction throw the day of Pentecost into the shade.

FIRST UNIVERSAL BISHOP — APOSTOLIC SUCCESSION.

The autocracy of the papal power culminated when Boniface III. was appointed universal bishop. In the early part of the seventh century, Pope Boniface III. was appointed to that position, not by Peter or any of his successors in the church of Christ — not by election in any ecclesiastical body — not by any people — but by that pious fraud Phocas, an unmitigated tyrant and usurper, whose crimes were of the darkest dye, an unfortunate link in the chain of claimed apostolic succession. This is by no means the only break in that chain, for looking into the history we find in the eleventh century that the papal chair was vacant one year, after being occupied by a boy ten years old, and thrice driven from the throne — again in the thirteenth century there was no Pope for three years, and at another time in the same century the papal chair was vacant for two years and three months — in the fourteenth century eleven months at one time and two years at another, during which the cardinals were quarrelling for the position. If such be the "unbroken *chain* of apostolic succession" the protestant church is in no immediate danger of strangulation by it.

CONTEST FOR WEALTH AND POWER.

From the days of Constantine in the fourth century to those of Boniface III. in the seventh, and Innocent III. in the thirteenth, there was a continual contest for wealth and power between Popes and Emperors, Archbishops and Kings, church and state. When death vacated a throne, and the hereditary heir was in his minority, it afforded an opportunity for the opposing power to gain the ascendency. In some cases the empire was in the ascendant, but more frequently the church. During these centuries the papal power had claimed one prerogative after another, until the contest culminated in the autocracy of the Pope, and Kings and Emperors alike lay at his feet, the victims of an absolute and irresponsible power. The chief points which the Pope claimed as his exclusive prerogative were

1. General supremacy of jurisdiction; a claim, it is obvious, absolutely illimitable.

2. Right of legislation, including the summoning and presiding in councils.

3. Judgment in all ecclesiastical causes, arduous and difficult. This includes the power of judging on contested elections, and degrading bishops, a super metropolitan power.

4. Right of confirmation of bishops and metropolitans, the gift of the pallium. Hence by degrees, rights of appointment to devolved sees, reservations, &c.

5. Dispensations.

6. The foundation of new orders.

7. Canonization.

A FEUDAL SOVEREIGNTY — HALF SPIRITUAL, HALF TEMPORAL.

In addition to the above claims or included in them, were many others established from time to time, to complete a feudal sovereignty, half spiritual and half temporal. Every monarchy in Europe had, one after another, become mere fiefs of the see of Rome. The supreme Pontiff of Rome was the God of earth. Practically, the God of heaven, the King of Kings and Lord of Lords — the Creator of all things in heaven and in earth, was a secondary power called upon only when necessary to strengthen the anathema of the Pope to bring rebellious Kings and Emperors into subjection to the church of which Innocent III. was the supreme pontiff at this time. His word was law; he claimed the power to forgive the sins of the greatest criminals, (or make them damnatory through all eternity) provided the criminal had wealth enough to satisfy the rapacity of the holy fathers and would cast it into the yawning maw of mother church. He could legitimatize the bastards of licentious kings and make them legal heirs to the crown, at a moderate price. He could grant absolution from all the sins of time, and also eternal happiness to any prostitute or undivorced queen, who could pay. He could not tolerate marriage among his clergy, but could allow them, what most of them accepted as a substitute, free rein and uncontrollable license in the convents. There was no gulf fixed between the monasteries and convents that could not be passed with impunity and the cases of moral purity in either were the exceptions rather than the rule.

He could dispense crowns and kingdoms or withhold them for a higher bid, by declaring them feudatory to the see of Rome. We might quote pages, but will give a single specimen on the latter point. Pedro, king of Aragon in Spain, a descendant of Charlemagne, conceived a passion for the rich and beautiful Maria, but as she was already the wife of Count Comminges, to whom she had borne two children, and as the Count had two wives living at the time he married the said Maria, the matter seemed to be a little mixed. By an arrangement between Pedro and the pope the thing was easily done by constituting the kingdom of Aragon, a fief of the Roman see, and the annual tribute of two hundred gold pieces, to be paid by the said Pedro and his successors to the said Pope Innocent III. and his successors. Thus Pedro and Maria were constituted husband and wife. Both had lived in open violation of the seventh commandment, without the endorsement of the pope, but now with it. All the commandments of the decalogue were at his disposal, to be enforced or abrogated at his sovereign will and pleasure.

WEALTH OF MONASTERIES.

The way to this pinnacle of fame and power had been paved by Charlemagne, Hildebrand and others until it was easy to lay the capstone of the edifice. The monasteries, which in the earlier centuries were the receptacles of the poor had become rich. As they increased in numbers, rank and influence, they ignored more and more the humbler classes. Their rules gradually relapsed. Their narrow cells grew into stately cloisters, deserts into parks, hermits into princely abbots. They became great religious aristocracies — worldly without impregnating the world with a religious spirit. It took hundreds of years to teach monastic christianity that the way to subjugate the world was not to coop up a chosen few in high-walled and secure monasteries in order to subdue the world into one vast cloister. They seem never to have heard of Christ's simple method, "go ye into all the world and preach the gospel to every creature." It is certain they had never obeyed the command, if they had ever heard of it.

DEATH TO PREACH THE GOSPEL — CRUELTY TO HERETICS.

To preach the gospel or embrace it after the apostolic pattern was heresy, and a crime in the eye of the Latin church, punishable with death. The popes claimed to be the only authorized successors of Christ and the apostles, and yet they put to the torture any one outside of the Latin church who believed and preached as the apostles did. The hierarchy did not require a belief in the apostles' doctrine, but only in the "holy catholic church" and the pope. If they believed and served these, they could with impunity cut out the tongue, put out the eyes, draw and quarter or burn alive heretics, and be rewarded for their *amusement*. These things were repeatedly done by order of the pope and his legates. No temporal power without a powerful army at command dared oppose the edicts of the supreme head of the church, and no monastic order under Innocent III. recognized the democracy of christianity with two exceptions, to wit, St. Dominic and St. Francis, and those were received with coldness by the pope and tolerated for a short time only. The monasteries were said to be the poor-houses of the middle ages. The crusades and holy wars of the church were not defensive but offensive wars, inaugurated and carried on for a double purpose in the interest of the church, to wit, the conquest of heretics and plunder, and the increase of the church in numbers and wealth.

POPE INNOCENT IV. AND FREDERICK II. — CONTEST FOR POWER.

After the death of Innocent III. the contest for power and pelf was continued with redoubled fierceness and fury between Pope Innocent IV. and Emperor Frederick II. These two autocrats, the one spiritual, the other temporal, were neither of them content with the prerogatives which properly belonged to them, but each contended for the supreme power. If the pope had been satisfied to rule supreme in the church, and allow the emperor to do the same in the state, much bloodshed and war would have been avoided. But the haughty, rapacious, and implacable pope was not so easily satisfied. When charged with heresy, Frederick did not hesitate to burn heretics by the hundreds to prove that he himself was not a heretic, but a true believer in the canons of the church. When hard pressed by the papal power, his appeal to primitive christianity and the doctrines of the apostles, his promulgation of democratic laws, with justice and equity as their basis, were all master-strokes of policy to shake the fabric of medieval religion, and undermine the all-powerful hierarchy. The raising and equipment of armies and navies was a game that two could play at. Papal bulls, excommunications, and the dreaded anathemas from the vatican, were hurled at Frederick with lavish profusion, but in return Innocent IV. found an adversary that was not afraid to hurl them contemptuously back into his teeth, especially so when a powerful army stood ready to vindicate imperial power.

BONIFACE VIII. — PHILIP THE FAIR — EDWARD I. PAPAL DESPOTISM.

In the last decade of the thirteenth century the strife for the mastery between the temporal and spiritual powers still raged, but between different parties. The insatiate maw of the Romish church had already gobbled up half the wealth of Europe, and her cry was still give, give. Boniface VIII. was a despot hard to match among kings and emperors. As supreme head of the church, the forgiver of sins, the peddler of absolutions, the granter of eternal happiness, and God on earth, he had had no superior if any equal. He even surpassed his predecessors in his rapacious claims of the revenues of empires and kingdoms, as well as the prerogatives we have specified. At the jubilee of the centennial, the abject submission of christendom would indicate that the representative of St. Peter had reached the zenith of his fame, perhaps of the Roman pontificate. His ruling passions were intoxicated, his ambition tempted, his pride swelled and his avarice glutted by the immense treasures laid at his feet by millions of worshippers from all parts of Europe.

War between France and England had caused the two haughty monarchs, Philip the Fair and Edward I. to demand of the clergy a portion of their revenues, to improve their exchequers and enable them to carry on the war. The pope interfered, and the contest was fierce. In the second year of his pontificate Boniface VIII. made a bold strike to sever the property of the church from all secular obligations. He issued a bull declaring himself " the one exclusive trustee of all the lands, goods, and properties held throughout christendom by the clergy, by monastic bodies, even by universities; and that without his consent no aid, benevolence, grant, or subsidy could be raised on their estates or possessions by any temporal sovereign in the world." Nor was this all. " No tax was to be levied on any property of the church, without the distinct permission of the pope." The penalty of taxing or receiving taxes was excommunication and the denial of absolution until the hour of death, and for paying taxes, on the part of the clergy, deposition was the penalty.

On the other hand, the kings of France and England, each for himself and in his turn, dealt some stunning blows to the whole papal despotism. The wealth of the church enabled the pontiff of Rome to make war or peace, according to his sovereign will and pleasure. Neither king could see it his duty to defend his realm against an enemy (and, of course, protect the treasures of the church within his realm), and lay the whole burden of the war upon the temporal power. As the church held so large a portion of property it was but fair for the hierarchy to pay their proportion of government expenses for protecting it. Accordingly they demanded a quarter to half of the annual income of the clergy. King Edward, as an offset to the bull of the pope, took into his own hands the administration of temporal affairs, shut the courts against the clergy, and declared "that those who would not contribute to the maintenance of the temporal power, should not enjoy its protection." Philip also struck the popedom in its most vital and sensitive part. "If the clergy might not be taxed for the exigencies of France, nor might in any way be tributary to the king, France would no longer be tributary to the pope." He also prohibited the export of gold, silver, and other articles to Rome, and proscribed bankers and other agents from transmitting papal revenues to Rome.

These papal bulls on the one side and kingly edicts on the other are simply specimens of others which are too long for this article. Boniface VIII. began to realize that the two kings were more than a match for him, and found it necessary to modify his next bull in several essential particulars. The bold and defiant tone of Philip, his sound logic, and appropriate quotations of scripture to sustain his positions, placed the clergy of his realm in a position to choose whom they would serve, the king or the pope.

The pope thought it not prudent to contest these broad and bold principles of temporal supremacy, and run the risk of losing his power over his own clergy and impairing his reserves.

Edward saw a cloud rising in Scotland too portentious to be neglected. The exchequer of both kings had become depleted. Neither the pope nor either potentate could maintain the lofty airs he had assumed, and the way was paved for a treaty between Philip and Edward. Boniface saw his opportunity to act as mediator and save his own dignity at the same time. A treaty was arranged between the contending armies of France and England and the centennial was celebrated as we have already related.

Soon after the centennial jubilee, the disputed prerogatives of the temporal power were again usurped by the ecclesiastical. Pope Boniface VIII. issued his bulls with an unsparing hand against the king of France and in quick succession, while Philip the Fair paid him back in edicts equally severe and mandatory. It was "diamond cut diamond," and so continued until 1303, when the supreme pontiff was summoned to the bar of that God whose prerogatives he had usurped during his whole pontificate. No previous pope had been summoned to the judgement to answer for a catalogue of darker crimes. According to the testimony of many witnesses, " the works of the flesh " enumerated by Paul in the fifth chapter of Galatians, attached to the supreme head of the *infallible* church of Rome, but none of the " fruits of the spirit." From the death of Boniface to that of his successor, Clement v., in 1314, the popedom had a most precipitous fall, after which its ruling influences were more subtle than powerful.

The successors of St. Peter and Cæsar were about equally sordid and corrupt. Philip the Fair of France was permitted to curse the world for more than a decade after the death of Boniface viii. with Clement v. as a vassal and supple tool. He succeeded in extinguishing the order of Knights Templars for the sake of their immense wealth. The temporal, assisted by the ecclesiastical power, put to the torture and burned at the stake all of that order who would not renounce their principles, and those who did renounce, and who acknowledged crimes they had never committed were kept in dungeons to drag out a miserable life. In either case their *property* was confiscated to the state or the church, or both, whose covetousness was not only not satisfied but whetted for a contest for the whole, in which the pope was more successful than the king. Both Clement v. and Philip iv., however, were summoned to the judgement-seat of Christ within a few months of each other during the same year, 1314. The pope dedicated his vast estates and ill-gotten gains, not to the church, but to nepotism, and the king squandered his share of the spoils and died a miserable bankrupt. The church, under the rule of Clement v., was said to have gone headlong to ruin. The hierarchy had reached the maximum of her power only to be hurled down to a proper level. The house of Philip was speedily and mysteriously extinguished as a condign retribution for his extortions, cruelties, and barbarities. Nor could his sons, with each an adulteress for a wife, long delay the penalty for his and their crimes.

POPE JOHN XXII. — CONTEST FOR POWER CONTINUED.
GOD AND MAMMON COMBINED.

The successors of Clement v., and especially John xxii., continued the strife for the temporal power, which became a leading topic of the controversy. The spiritual democracy began to be more bold in their opposition to the claims of the avaricious and godless hierarchy. Pope John xxii. held "that Christ, immediately on his conception, assumed universal temporal dominion." He forgets Christ's answer to Pilate, " My kingdom is not of this world, if my kingdom were of this world then would my servants fight." One of the late papal edicts claims that the " pope alone promulgates law; he alone is absolved from all law. He sits alone in the chair of the blessed St. Peter, not as mere man but as man and God. His will is law; what he pleases has the force of law."

Pope John xxii. acknowledged no higher power than himself in heaven, earth, or hell. The laws of God were binding upon everybody but himself. Christ's command to " lay not up for yourselves treasures on earth," was entirely disregarded, as may be seen by an inventory of his "treasures" after death, amounting to nearly seven and a half millions of dollars in coin (eighteen millions gold florins), and half as much more in gold and silver vessels. The depth of his piety may be judged of by the manner in which he obtained these " treasures." There does not appear to be any regular scale of prices for bishoprics, crowns, kingdoms, pardons (for sins against the Pope or church, called *absolutions*), but all these were sold with impunity, at prices limited only by the wealth of the subjects.

No wonder Pope John repudiated the poverty of Christ, as well as his divinity. To believe in the divinity of Christ and follow in his footsteps was the quintessence of heresy, for which the fire and faggot of the inquisition was the only remedy, and the confiscation of vast estates to the pope's treasury the result. Infallible Pope! Supreme Head of the Holy Catholic Church! Successor of St. Peter! Vicar of Christ! God on Earth!

In the eighth decade of the fourteenth century the supreme pontificate was re-established at Rome. During seventy years, the papal throne had remained at Avignon, and on the return of the autocrat of the church to Italy, a schism broke out and an effort was made to establish the supreme power of the church in the hierarchy instead of the pope. The conclave of cardinals at the council of Pisa, who had the right to make a pope had the right to depose him for cause, and commence the reformation of the church at its head. During this century a powerful adversary of the whole hierarchical system had appeared in England. John Wycliffe, the first apostle of Teutonic christianity or at least the harbinger, sowed seeds of the democracy of christianity which shook the dominion of the hierarchy, and led to the emancipation of mankind from sacerdotal and from Latin christianity. We have seen the fruits of this seed in the fifteenth and sixteenth centuries. John Wycliffe could tear down the old structure of sacerdotal christianity, better than he could make a new one to take its place. He seemed more successful at destruction than reconstruction, but perhaps if his life had been prolonged, he would have demonstrated to the world that he could not only tear down but build up. As it was, he laid bare the foundation stones of Christ and his apostles, for his successors to build upon, and in removing the sacerdotal rubbish under which the foundation stones of the *true* gospel structure had been buried for more than a decade of centuries, he paved the way for the Reformation.

JOHN HUSS — JEROME OF PRAGUE — JOHN XXIII.
BENEDICT XIII. — GREGORY XII.

In the fifteenth century the autocracy of the papal power received a still heavier blow. After the sudden death of Wycliffe, by paralysis, his mantle seemed to fall upon John Huss and Jerome of Prague, two Bohemian reformers, who ignored the infallibility of the pope and the church with their blasphemous teachings, and drank in the pure doctrines of Christ and his apostles. Of course this was heresy according to the canons of the church, and they were burned at the stake, by a decree of the Council of Constance. But the preaching of these men and their associates, in the providence of God, and in spite of the fire and fagot, had made an impression upon christendom, that the same council was constrained to heed in another case of very different character.

Pope John XXIII. had far exceeded all his predecessors in corruption and crime. As corrupt as Latin christianity had become, he had gone still deeper into all sorts of vices, and while he might not have added to the catalogue of crimes of his predecessors, he perpetrated them with even more boldness and defiance. The voluptuousness of his cardinals and bishops was commensurate with his own, and hence his immunity from crime. To condemn him was to condemn themselves, and vice versa. The council of Pisa which elected John XXIII. to the popedom, deposed two other popes to wit, Benedict XIII. and Gregory XII. and thus established a dangerous precedent, which the reform party in favor of the reformation of the hierarchy made good use of. The power of the cardinals not only to make popes but unmake them, was no longer successfully contested.

COUNCIL OF CONSTANCE — POPE JOHN XXIII. DEPOSED. CARDINAL'S HAT.

At the council of Constance, five years later than that of Pisa, which continued three years and a half, the reform party had the sagacity to see that one thing only could be done at a time, consequently the transfer of the supreme power from the pope to the council of the cardinals, with the council of Pisa as a precedent, was not impossible. The corruption of a long line of popes had made this step of paramount importance as a stepping-stone to other reforms which would strike at the vitals of the sacerdotal system. The damaging charges brought before the council of Constance against Pope John XXIII. and supported by undoubted testimony laid the foundation for his deposition from the papal throne "He had been guilty from his youth, and during his whole life, of the foulest crimes — a priest of licentiousness which passes belief, promiscuous concubinage, incest, the violation of nuns; of the most atrocious cruelties, murder, massacre, the most grinding tyranny, unglutted avarice, unblushing simony." Yet for all these crimes the conclave which was composed of twenty-three cardinals and thirty delegates from the council, politely waited upon this mass of moral putrefaction down the steps of the papal throne, to receive a cardinal's hat at the hands of his successor whom they were about to appoint. The same council condemned to the fire and the fagot John Huss and Jerome of Prague for preaching the doctrines, pure and simple, of Christ and His apostles, and for exemplifying the christian graces in their lives, not stained with crime. The reason why Pope John was not condemned to the gallows or the stake, was because the conclave and the pope were all in the same boat. The *crimes* of the fifteenth century were the *graces* of the Latin church ; and the christian *graces* of the first century had become crimes in the fifteenth.

LUTHER AND THE REFORMATION.

In the sixteenth century when Martin Luther came upon the stage of action, he found the great highway to the Reformation already graded and the track laid, by John Wyckliffe, John Huss and others in the fourteenth and fifteenth centuries. The way was thus prepared for him to roll on the car of emancipation from sacerdotal religion. Wyckliffe and Huss attacked the *practices,* while Luther first attacked the *doctrines* of Rome, and subsequently her practices. He struck the key note of the Reformation when he nailed his ninety-five theses to the door of the church at Wittenberg. In demolishing the sale of indulgencies he struck at the vitals of the papal system without intending it. After he had belled the cat, he said " the tune was nearly too high for my voice." The theses, like the cry of fire in a populous city, aroused all Germany, and in one short month was carried across the Alps and rung in the ears of the vatican. Luther was now in a position to defend himself.

At twenty years of age he had dug out of the rubbish of the university at Erfurth, an old moth-eaten bible in the Latin language, of which he was then master, the first one he ever saw in his life. In it was revealed to him the doctrines of Christ and His apostles, which had been concealed from the world by the popes and their satellites for a dozen centuries. The clear foundation doctrines of the christian religion shined from its pages in a striking contrast to vaticanism. Justification by faith, the terms of human salvation by grace, "repent and believe on the Lord Jesus Christ and thou shalt be saved," and other fundamental doctrines which cut up popery by the roots, were a perfect surprise to him.

He determined to go down to the foundation of the whole system of christianity, and to this end he learned the Hebrew and Greek languages that he might get at the true meaning of scripture, and make a translation of the Bible into the German language. This translation was made in due time and sent into the German families; and as no traces of the hierarchical system could be found in it, papacy was put upon its own merits. Luther had not yet purposed to overthrow the primacy of Rome, and counted it and catholicism on his side in dealing with the mammon worshippers among the barefaced monks, among whom were Tetzel, the great auctioneer for the sale of indulgences, and a still more powerful opponent, and former friend, Dr. Eck, the sturdy scholastic gladiator.

The most important step of all — the translation of the New Testament into the vulgar tongue — made short work with the corrupt practices of the papacy and shook the doctrines of Antichrist from centre to circumference. While the civil powers, by authority of the papal, were burning the new translation in bonfires, all Germany was ablaze with a moral fire which substituted the marriage of the New Testament for the celibacy of the priesthood in the canons of the church, liberty of conscience for monastic vows, the Lord's supper for transubstantiation, repentance towards God for penance to the priest, salvation by the grace of God through faith in Jesus Christ's atonement, for the sale of indulgences and salvation by works.

The superstitions of Rome, and the subtle and pedantic systems of the schoolmen, melted away before an honest translation of the Bible, like error before truth. Those scattered stones which Luther had so laboriously hewn from the quarries of Scripture were now combined into the majestic edifice of christianity, which neither pope, nor cardinal, nor king, nor emperor, nor all the devils in hell could overthrow.

Luther soon found that his contemplated reforms could not be, after all, accomplished, until the papal power was broken. The christian religion and the hierarchical system were antipodes and one or the other must be destroyed. In bidding farewell to Rome, he wrote a long letter to Pope Leo x. in which he says, " the church of Rome, once the foremost in sanctity, is become the most licentious den of robbers, the most shameless of all brothels, the kingdom of sin, of death and of hell which Antichrist himself, if he were to appear, could not increase in wickedness. All this is clearer than the sun at noonday; once it was the gate of heaven, now it is the mouth of hell."

In the same letter of divorcement from the church of Rome, he quotes from Rev. 22; 11, his authority for the step, as follows: " He that is unjust, let him be unjust still; and he which is filthy let him be filthy still." He also tells the pope that " to be a christian, is not to be a Roman." In examining the original Greek he found that the Latin church had committed a fraud by substituting *penance* for *repentance* the real meaning of the original. The former is the main-spring of the man-made papal system, while the latter is one of the fundamental doctrines of the God-made christian religion. The one is a human expiation to the pope, the other a transformation or conversion of the heart to God.

The twenty days disputation at Leipsic between the reformers and the Roman hierarchy in 1519, settled the question with Luther. It was God's word against human traditions. He had unmasked vaticanism in its corrupt practices, in his thesis alluded to, and now he and his friends demolish the whole fabric of human traditions (which constitute the papal system), with the word of God. He calls the pontifical law " the nest of every heresy."

In 1520 Luther attacked the papal powers as the great Antichrist of the Bible, and proceeded to strip the sovereign pontiff Leo x. of his stolen wealth and usurped prerogatives. It did not take the Wittenberg doctor many months to learn from the prophecies of Daniel and St. John, and from the Epistles of St. Paul, St. Peter and St. Jude, that the papacy was and is the Antichrist of the Bible.

1522, Sep. 21. The New Testament was published in German, at Wittenberg. and 3000 copies in two folio volumes, — a translation from the original by Martin Luther, assisted by Melancthon, — were sold at a moderate price. Three presses were employed, says Luther, and 10 000 sheets were printed daily. The first edition was sold, and a second edition issued in December. In 1533 there had been printed seventeen editions at Wittenberg, thirteen at Augsburg, twelve at Basle, one at Erfurth, one at Grimma, one at Leipsic, and thirteen at Strasburg. Luther began the Old Testament translation in 1522, and issued it in parts to satisfy the demand of the people.

Scripture led man to faith, and faith led him back again to Scripture. These two principles combated two fundamental errors. Faith was opposed to the Pelagian tendency of Roman catholicism; scripture to the theory of tradition and the authority of Rome, (see D'Aubigne, p. 357.) Henry VIII., king of England, denounced the work, and all the states devoted to Rome ordered Luther's Bibles to be gathered into the hands of the magistrates ready for the torch. Among the obedient states were Duke George of Saxony who lead satan's forces, Bavaria, Brandenburg and Austria. Bonfires were made of these sacred books in public places. See page 338, Ib.

The staircase of the Reformation was ascended step by step and the errors of Rome were abolished one by one by the reformers.

In the churches in Saxony the reformers rejected the abuse and restored the use of the ministry and the sacraments. In regard to the advances of the Reformation in Germany, A. D., 1516 to 1529, D'Aubigne says, page 513; " In every place, instead of a hierarchy seeking its righteousness in the works of man, its glory in external pomp, its strength in material power, the church of the apostles reappeared, humble as in primitive times, and like the ancient christians, looking for its righteousness, its glory, and its power solely in the blood of the Lamb, and in the Word of God."

" The jurisprudence of Rome," says D'Aubigne, p. 578, " consisted, according to a prophecy uttered against the city which *is seated on seven hills*, in adorning itself with pearls that it had stolen, and in becoming drunk with the blood of the saints." See Rev., chapters 17 and 18.

Evangelical christianity established itself in Germany in 1530. Legal protestantism was definitely established in 1555, at the Diet of Augsburg, which was intended by the papacy to crush it, the former was that of the Word of God and of faith, the latter that of the sword and diplomacy. See D'Aubigne, p. 595.

" All the European states," says D'Aubigne, (page 608) that have embraced the reformation have been elevated, while those which have combated it have been lowered."

LOUIS XIV. — THE HUGUENOTS — EDICT OF NANTES REVOKED — THE INQUISITION — PERSECUTION OF PROTESTANTS — BIBLES BURNED — CRUELTIES PRACTICED — ESTATES CONFISCATED.

During the last half of the seventeenth century the autocracy of the papal power was more fully developed in catholic France under the reign of Louis XIV. by the wholesale massacre and exile of the Huguenots. The enraged hierarchy had witnessed the decline of their power, both temporal and spiritual in England, Ireland, Scotland, Germany, Switzerland, Netherlands, &c., &c., and something must be done to exterminate heresy or all was lost. It was every where patent that the losses of popery were the gains of protestantism. It was also evident to all the world that the union of the temporal and spiritual powers in one supreme head, had repeatedly proved a failure, that the inquisition with all the fiendish tortures the Jesuits could invent was making protestants quite as fast as it destroyed them, and that neither policy had as yet proved a remedy for heresy. — Therefore another grand effort must be made to revive the drooping spirits of the papacy and fill up the churches. For this bloody work Louis XIV. was the right man in the right place. The tolerating edict of Henry IV. (edict of Nantes) was revoked, for which Louis was applauded by all the fiends in human shape. Te Deums were sung at Rome in thanksgiving by Pope Innocent XI.

If there were no jubilees in hades it was because the morals of its inhabitants were purer than the papal church of Europe. For sixty years after the revocation of the edict of Nantes, France was said to be "a perpetual St. Bartholomew." The property of the 1,800,000 Protestant *families* was confiscated and made free plunder for the lascivious soldiery and scarcely less corrupt priesthood. "More than one million Frenchmen either left the kingdom or were killed, imprisoned, or sent to the galleys in their efforts to escape. In Languedoc alone, "besides those who succeeded in making their escape, the province lost not fewer than one hundred thousand persons by premature death, the sword, strangulation and the wheel." After thirty years of robbery, murder and carnage the *pious* "Louis xiv. proclaimed that there were no Protestants whatever in France, that Protestantism had been entirely suppressed." It had indeed been suppressed by law, but many fled to the deserts and hid away "in caves, valleys, moors, woods, old quarries and hollow beds of river," so that, one hundred years later than the revocation, when Louis xvi. granted them an edict of tolerance, there were "two millions useful citizens" in France.

But why should the Huguenots flee to their hiding places after the revocation? The proclamations, laws and edicts of Louis xiv. will answer that question. During the persecutions before the revocation, many families who had estates sold them for the most they could get and left the country with the proceeds. This was a rich harvest for speculators, as they could buy the estate of a heretic at their own price.

But after the revocation, heretics had no rights that papists were bound to respect. The edict of revocation proclaimed that "every Huguenot subject must be of the king's religion." To worship "*publicly* after their own religious forms, the penalty was death," to worship "in their own homes *privately*," the penalty was "the galley for life." They were forbidden under heavy penalties to even look out of their own windows, while a catholic procession was passing, bearing the corpus domini, but must hang out a flag. It was five hundred livres fine to neglect to send a child to be baptized and brought up in the Roman catholic faith. The boys were educated in the Jesuit schools and the girls in the nunneries. Their parents were obliged to pay the bills while their funds lasted, and after they were sufficiently fleeced their children were turned over to the general hospitals where no ray of protestant light could reach them. Every child of five years old was forcibly taken possession of by the catholic authorities and removed from its protestant parents, the result of which was often death to one or both. Every protestant temple in France was legal plunder, and the pastors had fifteen days to leave the country, or be sent to the galleys if found preaching Christ and Him crucified in that time, but if found after the fifteen days lingering in France, his portion was death. Protestant marriages were illegal and their children bastards. Doctors of both sexes were forbidden to practice; apothecaries were suppressed, schools were abolished, groceries closed, all offices were denied them, and they were not even allowed to work on the public roads. Bibles, testaments and all other religious protestant books were collected and publicly burned in every town In Metz the bonfire lasted a whole day. The collections deposited with the catholic clergy furnished the fuel.

Protestant housekeepers were liable to be sent to the galleys for life for hiring a protestant servant, even a "new convert." All these and every other insult and degradation that could be fished up from the bottomless pit were perpetrated upon these poor Huguenots, who refused "to be of the king's religion." Bribery was another means used to convert the higher classes. Pastors were offered higher salaries, and judges were offered as high as six thousand livres as a pension. Every pastor taken at the meetings of the peasantry was hung, and a reward of five thousand five hundred livres was offered for every pastor who should be taken at a meeting, and the penalty of death was awarded to those who should attend any of them. The cruelties practiced under these laws and edicts upon an unoffending and religious people are almost incredible. The recital of their details can be endured only by persons of the strongest nerves and will therefore be omitted.

Catholic France of the seventeenth century is the legitimate offspring of the Roman catholic church. The persecutions of protestant christians were the natural fruits of her teaching. All up through the middle ages her conversions were by might and power not "by my spirit saith the Lord." The medieval church, under the long line of profligate popes was made up of the most unsanctified wretches the world ever produced. God took good care to put into it salt enough to start the reformation, from her own ranks, and also to raise up the men to conserve and propagate true piety.

Let us not be deceived in the character of the institution we are to deal with. We shall soon see that the question which more than any other seems to claim the attention of the old world, is one of supremacy between the civil and ecclesiastical powers, the temporal and the spiritual, the state and the papal church. In some localities it assumes the ecclesiastical form and becomes a contest between papists and protestants. In either form it is not a *new* question. For nearly fifteen centuries the papal power has striven for the mastery over both church and state, and for five centuries it has claimed *infallibility.* It has stolen the livery of heaven as its banner, and folded it under its autocratic robes as soon as its temporal power in any country was secured.

In this republic the sacerdotal robes of the papacy are worn in their most fascinating, submissive and obedient forms, and while it is quietly acquiring its civil supremacy all will be lovely; but turn the scale and put the civil power into its hands, and its autocrasy and despotism will soon be developed, as it always has been in other countries, as attested by history. God forbid that the iron rod of papacy should ever be extended over this country. "Eternal vigilance is the price of liberty."

The papacy also claims an unbroken succession from Christ and his apostles, and it audaciously claims the prerogatives of both Christ and Cæsar, by virtue of which it acquired the divine right to rule the world, civil and ecclesiastical. The pope's will is absolute over the bishops, the bishops over the priests, and the priests over the people. Add to this the temporal power and all the elements of an autocrat and despot center in the pope. His word *excathedra* is law from which there is no appeal, and whether fallible or infallible, it is the same for all practical purposes.

The papal church claims credit for preserving the scriptures through the medieval ages. It has a better claim to the infamy of destroying them, as we have already seen. God saved His bible from the devouring element, but no thanks to the papacy, as an organized power. God took care to raise up *individuals* who would hide away their bibles at the risk of losing their heads. Portions of the scriptures and some important links of history were exhumed from the ruins of old monasteries, and dug out of the rubbish of centuries, but they were the hidden treasures that escaped the argus eyes of the vatican, and an obedient priesthood.

In like manner the papal church claims the credit of bringing the world from a state of barbarism to civilization. from paganism to christianity. But *cui bono*. It only transfered the worst features of both to its own organization, intensifying their modes of torture many fold for its own advancement. At the gladiatorial combats when hated christians were thrown into the arena of the coliseum to be torn in pieces and devoured by wild beasts for the amusement of the people, the process was merciful when compared with the later contrivances of the hierarchy to dispose of and exterminate heretics, by the thumb-screw, the wheel, and other modes of slower torture used by the inquisition, too bad to mention here. Nor is it possible for the papal church to hide its true character under its sacerdotal robes of hypocrisy in this country. Our free schools, free press, free pulpits, with the liberty of speech, will unmask the great hypocrite and show her naked deformity as it has existed for centuries in the old world.

That the papal church is an *old* institution, and that it has had popes for many centuries may be all true, but that its popes are *infallible,* or that they form a true and unbroken line of succession from the apostles, or that they represent the *true* church of Christ and His apostles in any sense is not true, but emphatically denied by history.

The church of Christ is one of *moral,* while that of Rome is one of *physical* force, constituting a political organization of the worst type, as demonstrated the world over. But its *political* character will be discussed more fully in the third and fourth chapters of this pamphlet.

CHAPTER II.

VATICANISM IN THE NINETEENTH CENTURY.

Let us now turn to the history of our own times, and see whether the papal system as now practised with all the "modification" and "softening down" claimed for it, is an element in harmony with the civil powers of either Europe or America, the old world or the new.

1. GERMANY. In the lower house of the Prussian diet on the 16th of March, 1875, Prince Bismarck, in a speech on the new ecclesiastical bill, said, "the maxim that more obedience was due to God than to man, certainly did not mean that more obedience was due to the pope, misguided by Jesuits, than to the king." Subsequently the bill was passed, and some of its provisions were reported in the papers as follows:

"The contributions from the public treasury, for the support of the bishops, priests and institutions of the Roman catholic church, will be suspended until they submit to the laws of this state, until which the state will not compel the payment of dues to the bishops and clergy as heretofore." If the pope revokes the written pledges of his bishops and priests to obey the laws of the state, the same laws provide a severe penalty. Whether the other members of the confederacy follow Prussia's lead remains to be seen. Endowment is to be the reward of obedience. Bismarck's purpose is to destroy the pope's *secular* power in Germany, not to break up the *ecclesiastical* power of the German hierarchy. "In the upper house of the Prussian diet, on the 14th of April, the bill withdrawing the state grants from Roman catholic clergymen was under debate. Prince Bismarck made a speech in which he declared that since the vatican council, catholic bishops were merely the pope's prefects. He said that he was not an enemy to the catholic church. He warred only against papacy which had adopted the principle of extermination of heretics and which was in enmity with the gospel as well as with the Prussian state."

After informing the world that "the supreme cathedra of truth by divine dispensation was placed in Italy," the pope pathetically acknowledges that he is powerless. He bemoans his lost power, confirms his bishops in Germany in their "apostolic authority" and gives the fullest praise before the catholic world to the said bishops for their firm opposition to the civil power.

2. ENGLAND. In England the contest is waxing warm between the civil and papal powers, and an effort is made by archbishop (now cardinal) Manning, and a score of others to batter the edge of Mr. Gladstone's late pamphlet, in which he shows the world that civil obedience is incompatible with the demands of the vatican. No one denies that the Romanists may render tacit obedience to the civil power, when not in conflict with papal decrees. But all the world knows that when the occupant of St. Peter's chair commands one thing and the civil power the opposite, the pope must be obeyed by all papists, and not the civil powers. For more than a dozen centuries the head of the papal church has claimed the prerogative of vetoing the acts of all civil powers. Says Mr. Gladstone, "the papal church is in direct feud with the larger part of christendom to-day. In addition to those countries already named we may add from the list, Portugal, Spain, Switzerland, Austria, Russia, Brazil, and most of South America."

Mr. Gladstone charges "vaticanism with the intention of restoring the temporal sovereignty by foreign arms," and not a papal writer from cardinal Manning down, has yet denied it, but many glory in it. The revival of the ridiculous claim of "infallibility" within the last half decade, to say nothing of the ludicrous doctrine of the "Immaculate conception," is another loose spoke in the vatican wheel, but the rubber tire of the last allocution of the tottering occupant of St. Peter's chair, is inadequate to tighten the wheel. Contrasted with some of his predecessors such as Boniface III. in the seventh century, Innocent III. of the thirteenth, Boniface VIII. of the fourteenth, and John XXIII. of the fifteenth, to say nothing of many others, the present pope is a saint. The loss of his temporal power in some countries, and its only partial retention in others, together with his decaying health have somewhat toned down his last allocution, in which mandatory decrees give place to humiliating confessions of weakness. This may be pardoned in a superannuated old man, but his successor may be a very different sort of a man to deal with.

The animus of the hierarchy has been substantially the same for fifteen hundred years. The next pope may be a very good man or a very bad one, and it behooves the United States to prepare for the worst. The society of Jesuits has been, for many years sending its members to this country, until they are as thick as blackberries. The members of this society are ineligible to the office of bishop, cardinal or pope, but they are the most obsequious devotees of the vatican, the best material for inquisitions, and the most dangerous element of all the priesthood in the civil powers of the world, because better educated. They call themselves the society of Jesus, but the society of Judas Iscariot would be more appropriate. All newspaper readers know that the protestant governments of Europe have for years past been trying to rid themselves of this mortal foe of civil liberty, as for example the Prussian diet, already alluded to, a year or two since banished the whole crowd from its territory and gave six months for compliance. The bishops protested in the interest of the Jesuits, and the pope applauded them for their opposition to the heretical government.

3. ITALY. We cheerfully admit that there are many worthy members of the papal church in this country, but they are ignorant of the historical facts we are now considering, while others who are better posted, do not believe the histories by their own authors, when quoted by protestants. For the special benefit of that class of persons, we will call their attention to priest-ridden Italy of the nineteenth century. Within the last decade she has become an independent state. During sixteen hundred years she has groped in the midnight of priestly superstition. The papal church has there had a fair opportunity to give the world a specimen of what she could do for it. She has grasped the wealth of the nation and deposited it in the closets of her hundred cathedrals, for the princely support of her army of priests, while one-half the people know not to-day where they are to get bread for to-morrow. Says a late traveller, "There are thousands of churches in Italy, each with untold millions of treasures stored away in its closets, and each with its battalion of priests to be supported. And then there are the estates of the church, league on league of

the richest lands and the noblest forests in all Italy, all
yielding immense revenues to the church, and none paying
a cent in taxes to the state. In some districts the church
owns *all* the property, lands, warehouses, woods, mills and
factories. They buy, they sell, they manufacture, and since
they pay no taxes, who can hope to compete with them?"

4. FRANCE. A few years since the Romish priests
made an effort to procure an act of the general assembly of
France restoring to the clergy the entire instruction and
control of the national schools as had been the case before
the time of Napoleon Bonaparte. In these schools as nothing was taught except the creed and the elements of the
papal faith, the emperor changed the system entirely and
removed the priests from the schools, whom the Bourbons
subsequently restored. The last revolution, however, re-
lieved the schools from papal rule, and the effort of the
priests as above stated brought out the following speech in
the general assembly, from the gifted and eloquent Victor
Hugo, the foremost intellect of France.

"Ah, we know you! We know the clerical party. It is
an old party. This it is, which has found for the truth
those two marvellous supporters, ignorance and error! This
it is, which forbids to science and genius the going beyond
the Missal, and which wishes to cloister thought in dogmas.
Every step which the intelligence of Europe has taken, has
been in spite of it. Its history is written in the history of
human progress, but it is written on the back of the leaf.
It is opposed to it all. This it is, which caused Prinelli to
be scourged for having said that the stars would not fall.
This it is, which put Camanella seven times to the torture,
for having affirmed that the number of worlds was infinite,
and for having caught a glimpse at the secret of creation.
This it is, which persecuted Harvey for having proved the
circulation of the blood. In the name of Jesus, it shut up
Galileo. In the name of St. Paul, it imprisoned Christo-
pher Columbus. To discover a law of the heavens was an
impiety. To find a world was a heresy. This it is which
anathematized Pascal in the name of religion, Montaigne in
the name of morality, Moliere in the name of both morality
and religion. . . . For a long time already the human
conscience has revolted against you, and now demands of

you, 'What is it that you wish of me?' For a long time already you have tried to put a gag upon the human intellect. You wish to be the masters of education. And there is not a poet, not an author, not a philosopher, not a thinker that you accept. All that has been written, found, dreamed, deduced, inspired, imagined, invented by genius, the treasure of civilization, the venerable inheritance of generations, the common patrimony of knowledge, you reject.

" There is a book — a book which is, from one end to the other, an emanation from above — a book which is for the whole world what the Koran is for Islamism, what the Vedas are for India — a book which contains all human wisdom, illuminated by all Divine wisdom — a book which the veneration of the people call *The Book* — the Bible! Well, your censure has reached even that. Unheard-of thing! Popes have proscribed the Bible! How astonishing to wise spirits, how overpowering to simple hearts, to see the finger of Rome placed upon the book of God?

"And you claim the liberty of teaching. Stop ; be sincere; let us understand the liberty which you claim. It is the liberty of *not* teaching. You wish us to give you the people to instruct. Very well. Let us see your pupils! Let us see those you have produced. What have you done for Italy? What have you done for Spain? For centuries you have kept in your hands, at your discretion, at your school, these two great nations, illustrious among the illustrious. What have you done for them? I am going to tell you. Thanks to you, Italy, whose name no man, who thinks, can any longer pronounce without an inexpressible filial emotion; Italy, mother of genius and of nations, which has spread over the universe all the most brilliant marvels of poetry and the arts; Italy, which has taught mankind to read, now knows not how to read! Yes, Italy is, of all the states of Europe, that where the smallest number of natives know how to read.

"Spain, magnificently endowed; Spain, which received from the Romans her first civilization, from the Arabs her second civilization, from Providence, and in spite of you, a world, America; Spain, thanks to you, to your yoke of stupor, which is a yoke of degradation and decay, Spain has lost this secret power, which it had from the Romans; this genius of art, which it had from the Arabs; this world, which it had from God; and in exchange for all that you have made it lose, it has received from you — the Inquisition.

" The Inquisition, which certain men of the party try to-day to re-establish, which has burned on the funeral pile millions of men; the Inquisition, which disinterred the dead to burn them as heretics; which declared the children of heretics, even to the second generation, infamous and incapable of any public honors, excepting only those who shall have denounced their fathers; the Inquisition, which, while I speak, still holds in the papal library the manuscripts of Galileo, sealed under the papal signet! These are your masterpieces. This fire, which we call Italy, you have extinguished. This colossus, that we call Spain, you have undermined. The one in ashes, the other in ruins. This is what you have done for two great nations. What do you wish to do for France?

" Stop; you have just come from Rome! I congratulate you. You have had fine success there. You come from gagging the Roman people; now you wish to gag the French people, I understand. This attempt is still more fine; but take care; it is dangerous. France is a lion, and is alive!"

The above is taken from "The question of the hour," by Rev. Rufus W. Clark, who says: — Shall a Frenchman thus speak in France, and we be silent? Shall one, brought up amid papal influences, see so clearly the withering power of Romish education, and any person in this land of gospel light be blind to it?

Let us now leave Europe and cross the Atlantic ocean for North America, and learn the programme of the vatican for this country.

5. MEXICO. During the war of the slaveholders' rebellion in the United States, Napoleon III., Emperor of France, took it into his head that his opportunity had come to establish a government in Mexico after his own heart, without the risk of interference from the United States. Maximillan was said to be the right man in the right place. The probability was so strong that he would be the future emperor of Mexico, that Pope Pius IX. addressed the prince a letter,

which was published in Appleton's Annual Cyclopedia, 1865, p. 749, in which he says,

" Your majesty is well aware that, in order effectually to repair the evils occasioned by the revolution, and to bring back as soon as possible happy days for the church, the catholic religion must, above all things, continue to be the glory and the main stay of the Mexican nation, *to the exclusion of every other dissenting worship ;* that the bishops must be perfectly free in the exercise of their pastoral ministry; that the religious orders should be reestablished, or reorganized, conformably with the instructions and the powers which *we* have given; that the patrimony of the church, and the rights which attach to it, may be maintained and protected ; that *no person may obtain the faculty of teaching and publishing false and subversive tenets;* that instruction, whether public or *private,* should be directed and watched over by *the ecclesiastical authority;* and that, in short, the chains may be broken which, up to the present time, have held down the church in a state of dependence, and subject to the arbitrary rule of the civil government."

If this nice little scheme had succeeded the way would have been paved for the acknowledgement of the independence of the Southern Confederacy, and the pope would have got more credit for infallibility in leading off in that measure. Moreover with Maximillan to rule Mexico, by the grace of Napoleon III., and the pope to rule both, with the independence of the Southern Confederacy acknowledged, including slavery as its chief corner stone, how long think ye the American government would have withstood that storm of despotism ?

But diplomacy having failed in Mexico, the *ecclesiastical* mill was set in motion by the blood-thirsty representatives of the papal power, to grind up protestant missionaries for their blood, as farmers grind apples for their cider. We will give one or two specimens of this operation. The Rev. J. L. Stephens, a missionary of the American Board, at Ahualulco, Mexico, was murdered on Sunday, March 1, 1874. The telegram from the city of Mexico to the daily papers reads thus:

" In the morning a priest delivered an incendiary sermon, in the course of which he advocated the extermination of the protestants. This so excited his hearers that in the evening an armed mob of two hundred persons broke into the house of Mr. Stephens, and with cries "Long live the priest," smashed his head to jelly and chopped his body into pieces. They afterward sacked the house and carried off everything of value.

After much delay, the riot was suppressed by the local authorities. The Government has sent a detachment of troops to the place. A rigid investigation has been set on foot, and orders issued for the arrest of all priests in Ahualulco and the neighboring town of Teshitan."

Strange as it may seem the severest rebuke of this unprovoked and atrocious murder, we have seen, comes from the Boston Pilot, the Roman catholic organ for New England. The Pilot says, "should it turn out to be true, the crime of all the mob should be intensified on his head by a terrible punishment. The wretches who could kill a man with a religious cry on their lips, are the greatest wretches in the world." This is a perfect God-send to the timid protestant press, for they can copy Mr. Patrick Donahue's rebuke as an item of news, and a salvo to their own consciences for not doing their duty. The same papers inform us that " Rev. Antonio Corral was stoned and his chapel sacked in the city of Puebla, Mexico, on the 7th of March, by Roman catholics."

6. THE UNITED STATES.

THE PAPAL CHURCH AND THE FREEDMEN.

The efforts that have been made since the close of the war of the rebellion, to convert the freedmen, not to Christ, but to the papal church, stands in striking contrast to the efforts of that church, both before and during the war, to keep them in bondage. As *slaves* they were not wanted in the papal church, but as *voters* it is suddenly discovered that that is the very place for them. The motive for this movement on the part of the church, will appear, as we proceed, so perfectly transparent, that any mind of ordinary capacity will easily see and comprehend it. Having devoted the best twenty years of our own life and many thousand dollars to the anti-slavery cause, we cannot quietly stand by and witness this glaring hypocrisy without a note of warning. Having fitted for college under a Roman catholic priest, and been offered a collegiate course on condition of entering the priesthood, (which we declined,) and having been educated in the laws, tenets, canons and dogmas of the papal church we know wherof we affirm.

In the previous chapter we have deduced from the most authentic histories of nearly fourteen centuries the civil and ecclesiastical character of the institution under consideration, for the special benefit of the protestant church many of whose members have not access to that kind of literature, and cannot well spare the time to read it if they had.

The colored people having been so recently emancipated from the American slaveholding oligarchy, it would be a great calamity to allow themselves to be transferred to the Roman hierarchy. As in the former there were some kind masters, so in the latter there have been some kind popes. But in both cases they are the exceptions not the rule. The despotism lies in the system each represents. As the oligarchy requires the most despotic measures to keep its subjects in subjection, so the hierarchy requires the most despotic popes to rule the church of Rome. The present encumbent of St. Peter's chair is a superannuated old man, on the verge of the grave, who has beheld with tears, the temporal power of the old world sliding from under him, without the power to arrest the progress of the nineteenth century. In the slaveholders' rebellion the vatican was the only power on earth that acknowledged the independence of the Southern states, but as that was an ignominious failure, they are now endeavoring to utilize a combination of political and ecclesiastical elements which has been in progress for a long time, by transplanting to the new world a despotism of the old. The political elements are divided into two parties numerically, nearly equal, the ecclesiastical into two churches, protestant and papal. The protestant church is composed of individuals, each with a conscience under God, but amenable to no power on earth. He can read his bible and think for himself. His religion allows him liberty of conscience. Each individual is his own conscience-keeper, and must answer as an individual to God for his own sins, and no man or body of men can answer for him. As an organization it is strictly religious.

THE CHARACTER OF THE PAPAL SYSTEM UNCHANGED.

For the benefit of whom it may concern, we shall now show that the character of the papal system has never changed for the better in any essential particular, and that its modification in this republic is only temporary, and a necessary step to gain control of the civil power, as an engine of force with which to suppress protestantism.

1. ITS AFFILIATION WITH THE PRO-SLAVERY PARTY BEFORE THE WAR. ITS REWARDS AFTER.

The slaveholders of the south were the natural allies of the democratic party, and constituted its head, while its tail was in the north. The Roman catholic church was the natural ally of that party, and the price of its co-operation was the offices the party had in its power to bestow. If the Roman catholic voters should be eliminated from the democratic party, the skeleton of the party only would remain, a powerless wreck. During the dozen years of our sojourn in New York, previous to 1872, the following facts were published in the newspapers of that city, from time to time showing the proportion of city offices held by Roman catholics in the democratic party, to wit, sheriff, register, comptroller, city chamberlain, corporation counsel, police commissioner, president of the Croton board, acting mayor, president of the board of councilmen, clerk of the common council, clerk of supervisors, five justices of the court of record, all the civil justices, all the police justices but two, all the police court clerks, three out of four coroners, fourteen-nineteenths of the common council, and eight-tenths of the supervisors.

In the years 1869, 1870 and 1871, out of the monies raised by tax on the property of New York city, the records show that $1,396.389 were paid to Roman catholic institutions, and only $138.146 to protestant and Hebrew institutions combined. Thus the papists got over ninety per cent. of the appropriations, which is probably about the proportion of criminals and paupers they throw upon the state in return to be taken care of also by the tax-payers. The above figures are merely specimens, of which we could make an entire chapter.

2. ITS SYMPATHY WITH THE REBELLION — RESISTANCE OF THE DRAFT — NEW YORK RIOTS.

That the Roman catholic democrats were responsible for the riots which resisted the draft of 1863, in the city of New York, no intelligent man acquainted with the facts will deny. The civil power was then and there in the hands of the democratic party; Horatio Seymour, governor. The offices as above stated were nearly all held by Roman catholics, who acknowledge their allegiance to the vatican at Rome higher than any obligation to the civil power of this country. The state militia stationed in the city were in full sympathy with the municipal government, and part of the plan was to clean out the city of all "niggers and abolitionists." The colored people were hunted like wild beasts of the desert, and were seen flying for their lives in all directions, abolitionists were threatened by their enemies and warned by their friends, the Principia association was notified to close the doors of its office to save the block from conflagration; the publisher of the Principia declined to desert his post and was peremptorily informed that his house with many others was marked for destruction. In passing from his office in Williams street to his house on Twentieth street he was shot at by the mob in open day but not killed; in one evening he witnessed from his dwelling seven incendiary fires in the vicinity.

In a private correspondence Secretary Chase was kept informed of all these movements He was advised that if the President was depending upon the state militia to save New York, he was depending upon a broken staff. On the receipt of this information the government at Washington lost no time in sending thirty thousand troops into New York harbor, under a suitable general, who notified the democratic ringleaders, whose names he had obtained, that the riots must be stopped forthwith or their heads must come off. The general knew who he was talking to, and his auditors knew who was talking to them. Gov. Seymour addressed the rioters from the steps of the City hall as "my friends." Whether the pathetic address of the governor at the City hall, or the fire-flashes of the cross eyed general at the Fifth avenue hotel, or the thirty thousand troops in the harbor argument was the more potent we do not know, but one thing we do know, viz., the riots were stopped and the draft went on without further interruption.

3. ACKNOWLEDGEMENT OF THE INDEPENDENCE OF THE SOUTHERN CONFEDERACY BY THE POPE.

So strong was the feeling at the vatican in favor of the rebellion, and so intense the desire to see republican liberty crushed out and slavery extended over this continent, that the "pope," the "holy father," the "infallible head of the church," the "vicegerent of God on earth" hastened to acknowledge the independence of the Southern Confederacy, and set an example to the civil potentates of the world to follow. Not a civil ruler on the globe dared follow his example, but the democratic party of New York showed its gratitude for and its appreciation of such favors in various ways, to wit, —

GRATITUDE OF THE DEMOCRATIC PARTY OF NEW YORK IN COIN.

In 1866 the legislature of New York voted for Romish institutions $124,000, and only $4,000 to protestants and Jews combined. Whenever catholics hold the balance of power, protestants have to take the back seats. In the first half of 1867, New York city voted Romish institutions $120,000, and for two successive years, $30,000 were put into the "city levy tax bill," for the Romanists. In addition to this they held a lease of land on Fifth avenue valued at nearly $2,000,000, for a ground rent of one dollar a year, for ninety-nine years! This is the way the money of protestants is used to build up and strengthen the Roman catholic element in the democratic party; and the Boss Tweed crowd, including Samuel J. Tilden were responsible.

4. THE ROMAN CATHOLIC OPPOSITION TO OUR COMMON SCHOOLS. THE SUPPRESSION OF THE BIBLE DEMANDED AND ACCEDED TO IN SEVERAL STATES. TESTIMONY OF PAPAL PRIESTS.

The only *direct* issue the papal power has made with any part of our republican system, is with the common schools. They like the *system* well enough, but wish to reorganize it in the interests of the Roman catholic church. At the late " Roman catholic conference," held in St. Louis, Mo., Father Butler of Kansas "thought it should not be forgotten that the public schools of this country had served as a model for catholic parochial schools." But as at present organized with the reading of the protestant Bible, they were declared to be "a nuisance." Father Phelan of St. Louis, said "they would as soon send their children into a pest house as let them go to the public schools." Mr. Hawley, of Pennsylvania, said, "the catholics had gained a great victory in driving the Bible out of the public schools." As this victory has as yet been only partial and not general, the gentleman was a little too fast. But the object of driving the protesttant Bible out of the schools is to get the catholic Bible into them. The reason is that the all important features of the papal system are not to be found in the protestant Bible at all, nor in any other except a false translation. At the same conference to which we have alluded, Father Graham said " the purpose was to put in them the correct version of the Bible, and the catholic catechism." They forget that the protestants provide for the *religious* instruction of their own children in separate schools, and generously leave the common schools free from sectarian instruction, for the special benefit of the papists, infidels or any body else who don't believe the Bible. There is no objection to the catholics having as many parochial schools as they please, but when they attempt to convert our common schools into nurseries of the Roman catholic church, it is about time for Protestants to wake up.

In the eyes of Roman catholics our common schools, without the Douay Testament and the Roman catholic catechism, are the very fountains of corruption. In the conference to which we have already alluded, one of the "fathers" said, "the public men of America were educated in the public schools and were exhibitions of the system, and they were the most dishonest and corrupt of any country in the world. Men can steal in this country with impunity, provided the amount is large enough. That the children of the country go heels over head to the devil, must be attributed to the education they receive in the public schools, which does not fit them for the temptations of the world.

In these schools men of science are honored and eulogized, but the name of Jesus Christ is not allowed to be mentioned with reverence. These children turn out to be learned horse-thieves, scholastic counterfeiters, and well posted in schemes of deviltry."

That many of our public men are *corrupt* we sorrowfully admit, but that their common school education is the *cause* of their corruption we emphatically deny. If father Phelan's assertions were true, how happens it that three-quarters or seven-eighths of all our criminals are graduates from catholic institutions? If "the name of Jesus Christ is not allowed to be mentioned with reverence," whose fault is it? Protestants who put the Bible into the schools or Roman catholics who put it out? Protestantism which tolerates the reading of the Bible in the schools *without comment*, or popery which assumes Christ's prerogatives and demands the substitution of the Roman catholic Bible and catechism, which place an infallible pope at the head of the church instead of Christ? Is this audacious claim of his infallible holiness doubted? Read the letter of "Pio" to the "Emperor of Germany." In this letter we find the following claim among others, " Every one who has been baptized belongs to the pope." To this, Emperor William replies " our evangelical creed does not permit us to accept, in our relations to God, any other mediator than our Lord Jesus Christ."

In this country in the matter of the division of our common school funds, the question partakes of both politics and religion, for the real question after all, is whether the civil power shall open its treasury, as in Germany, and furnish the papal church with funds to educate its children in the dogmas and doctrines of that church, or whether it shall provide for the *religious* education of its own children, as the protestant churches do, to wit, from their own treasuries. If the papal church is not satisfied with our common school system as it evidently is not, the wide world is open to it to go where it can do better. It will never be permitted to demoralize our system of education and pervert the common school fund to educate us in popery, until Americans lose their senses.

The pope claims infallibility, the church of which he is the head claims infallibility, both claim supreme power over the state. This audacious usurpation has controlled, or attempted to control, every government on earth, and the infant republic of these United States need not hope to form an exception. We have already indicated their plan and their policy, showed with what pertinacity they have thus far pursued both for many years, and with what success their efforts have been crowned. We are not at all surprised that our religious press, so far as it is controlled by ex-ministers, should hesitate to grapple with so formidable a foe. For purity of life and honesty of purpose the ministers who have exchanged the pulpit for the editorial chair are not excelled by any class of persons in the community. But many lack one element in their character, which is indispensable in an ecclesiastical war with the papal power. That element is the Martin Luther back-bone.

So long as satan can keep the protestant press and pulpit quiet, just so long will the papal power be able to capture one political post after another, until protestantism lays powerless at its feet. The pulpit or the press which ignores politics as an element in religion, ignores one half the Bible, and denies the transforming power of the christian religion. By this we do not mean that christianity should be let down to the standard of the brood of political demagogues who are now a curse to the country, but that "politics" should be purified and raised to the standard of the christian religion. It is as much a man's duty to vote in the state as it is to pray in the church, and he who makes long prayers in the latter on Sunday, and votes for corrupt politicians on Monday, is either a dupe or a hypocrite.

From the foregoing pages it appears that the papal church is a politico-religious institution, which assumes to govern the world in its dual capacity. The political press of this country seems to wait for the protestant pulpits to grapple with it, because it is an ecclesiastical organization in their line; on the other hand the protestant pulpits with few exceptions, seem to turn it over to the tender mercies of the political parties, because it is a political institution in their line. Thus between the two elements of politics and religion, the great Antichrist is comparatively safe from attack let her do what she will. The cunning and intriguing hierarchy takes note of the situation and governs herself accordingly. She sees through her political glasses that she has already the balance of power between the two great political parties, and she has political wisdom enough to form an alliance with the minority party, first because it is a minority party, and second because their political instincts are in harmony with each other. This will be found demonstrated in the two following chapters, which, by request were published and pretty extensively circulated in separate tracts as campaign documents, in the Presidential campaign of 1876.

' In addition to the question of our common schools, which are marked for capture or destruction, rule or ruin, by the papal power, comes the question of our penal institutions, where the attempt is being made to substitute canon law for our own statute laws, the practices of monarchal governments for republican. The Rev. Joseph Cook, in his seventy-first lecture in Boston, March 26th, said that "the demand is secretly made, and in a letter lately published by a representative Romanist, (Daily Advertiser, March 22, 1877,) it is publicly made in Boston, as it often has been in New York and Cincinnati, that in each penal institution there should be two chaplains, after the manner of Austria or France; and, of course, the implication is that in America, as in Europe, both should be paid by the State. Yield to that demand, and you will have a division of your public criminal fund. What will come after that? It means a demand for the division of your school fund. It means a demand for the division of your church fund. It means a demand for the division of your eleemosynary fund. You will have to face all these questions that have given so much trouble in those countries where there are State churches. . . . . Romish ecclesiastics want their chaplains paid by the state. They must learn that they are not in Austria, France, Prussia or England. *America means that all religious sects, Romanists included, shall pay their own bills. To demand that a sectarian chaplain or schoolmaster be paid by the State is to act against the whole spirit of American law.*"

www.ingramcontent.com/pod-product-compliance
Lightning Source LLC
Chambersburg PA
CBHW021438090426
42739CB00009B/1531